On-page SEO

Optimise your website
for search engines
AND
readers

Lars Sundin

ISBN 978-91-983748-9-6

on-page-seo-book.com

Preface

This book is about the things you can do on your website to make it rank better in Google. It is intended for anyone who is responsible for producing content to a website and wants people to find it. It may be a personal blog, a small homepage or a big commercial website – the principles for on-page SEO are the same.

On-page SEO is a craft more than a science. But it is a data-driven craft and there is an element of analysis to it. In my opinion, this makes the writing even more satisfying than usual.

Contrary to most other kinds of writing, when you do on-page SEO, you get instant feedback on your writing. It comes in the form of improved Google rankings and more visitors to your site. When you are done with this book, I bet you will be rising early every morning to check your stats!

Another part of the fun is that the methods described here almost always lead to visible improvements. Admittedly, there is no absolute guarantee, and if a number of specific conditions coincide, your efforts may go more or less unrewarded by Google. But even in the few cases when this happens, you will have improved the content on your website, and it will probably perform better even if the Google stats are unimproved. With that said, in most cases when you search-engine optimise a web page, results will follow, and Google will give its love to the optimised page.

I hope you enjoy it, that you're prepared to put in the work, and that it will help your website fulfil its purpose!

Contents

Contents

On being found

So, you have built this wonderful, perfect website that will do good for the totality of mankind, or at least for your own wallet. You sit back and stare at your statistics dashboard, waiting for the numbers to surge. But nothing happens.

It's as if people don't know that your site is there. As if they don't know how good it is and what great use it will be to them. And of course, you're right. They don't know about it.

And, honestly, how would they know? How do you expect people to find your fantastic website? The world wide web is such a huge place, and there's no catalogue.

Let's go to yourself for answers. How do you yourself find stuff on the internet? I think I know the answer: you google it!
That's what others do too. They type something in Google and click on Search. When they look at the search result, will they find your site there? Probably not. Most likely, your new website is not visible in Google. It's not ranking.

And that's where Search Engine Optimisation comes in, or SEO. SEO is about being visible in Google. (There are other search engines, but in this book we focus on Google, which has a dominating position in many markets.)

The purpose of SEO is to make your web page visible on the internet by having it show up when people search in Google.

If they can't find you, you don't exist. The sympathetic "working without being seen" is not an option on the world wide web. If no one sees your site, it forfeits its purpose, regardless of what the purpose is. (Admittedly, you may want to use a site just to share private pics with your family, or share information within an organisation. Then you can do without SEO.)

Being found is not enough

But even if you manage to make your page visible in Google, you're not quite done.

Even if you make a successful SEO effort and your site starts showing up in the search results, little is won unless some of the Google users also click on your blue link and arrive at your site.

If your site shows up in the search results but no one clicks on the link to visit it, your SEO efforts are useless (more or less).

Apart from being seen, you also must convince users to click through from Google to your site. When people start doing this, your mission is complete. That's when your web traffic starts surging, and your site starts fulfilling its purpose, whatever that purpose might be.

Conversion in Google

Each time a user clicks on your blue link in a Google search result, you have successfully converted that person from a searcher to a visitor. This is called "conversion". (There are other types of conversion too, to be discussed later.)

It's not the number of Google views that counts. What counts is the number of visitors to your site that Google generates.

Conversion must be a natural, full-blown part of your SEO effort. Otherwise you will not be able to reap the fruits of this effort. It becomes a waste of money and/or time.

Click-Through Rate (CTR)

To measure a web page's conversion rate in Google, divide the number of clicks that the page gets in Google by the number of times the page was viewed in Google: Clicks/Views.

This quotient is called the Click Through Rate, or CTR. It's a measure of how converting your appearance in Google is. There are several ways to increase this conversion rate, which we'll be looking at later in this book.

Views x CTR = Traffic

If one million people see your site in Google, but only ten people click through to your site, your click-through rate is a lousy 1 in 100 000. It's pretty terrible.

If, instead, one hundred people see your site in Google's search results, and again ten people click through, your CTR is 0.1 – much better!

Or, sort of. The conversion rate is much better, but the number of visitors is the same. And this is what counts, remember?

Now, if you could keep a CTR of 0.1 while increasing the number of Google views to 1000, then your web traffic would surge to a smashing 100 visitors. Now we're talking!

Or, let's say your CTR goes down to 0.05 in the process. Even then, if the number of views increased to 10 000, your web traffic would go up to 500 visitors. Sometimes you have to give a little to win a lot.

As you see, SEO and conversion are two links on the same chain. To optimise your website traffic, you need to work with both SEO and conversion at the same time.

True conversion - Google isn't everything

We're still not done. We need to add yet another complication before we get down to practical advice on how to search engine optimise your web pages.

As we saw above, what counts for you as a website owner is not the number of Google views, but the number of visitors they generate.

But even the number of visitors is not what actually matters.

What really, REALLY matters, is the number of visitors who come to your site and then make a purchase. Or sign up for your newsletter, sign your petition for a good cause, or whatever kind of "business" or purpose your site has.

What good is it to you if 10 000 people come to your site every day, if none of them buys your book or signs up to your webinar? One buying customer is surely better than a thousand visitors just having a look?

Turning visitors into buyers is a form of conversion too. It's a conversion that takes place on your site, where you're in total control. Let's call it the "buy rate".

The buy rate

The buy rate could be the percentage of visitors who take the desired action, as we discussed above. But it might also be the average sum that your visitors spend on the site, if you're offering things of different value.

In this case, you need to consider not only which Google users will eventually buy your product, but also how much they will spend.

Maximising the buy rate is the purpose of the so called landing pages: ingeniously crafted, often copy-intense pages that help customers take that last step on their buying journey. That makes them push that Buy button. Or sign up for a daily horoscope, or whatever the purpose of your website.

Affiliates: converting the converted

For those of you who work as affiliates, there's yet another step on the long trip from being seen in Google to actually generating business. For you guys, converting in Google and then converting on your own site still isn't enough.

As an affiliate, you need to target Google users who will:

- click out from Google to your site, then
- click out from your site to your partner's site, and then
- click on your partner's Buy button.

It's in these people's Google searches you want to be visible, with a message that appeals to these people and convert them in all three stages. Anything else is just bounce rate.

Branding – the value of exposure

Contrary to what was said above, being seen actually does have a value per se. Each and every Google view is valuable in the sense that it makes people aware of your site and your product.

With this aspect in mind, maybe 10 000 views with a CTR of 0.1 is actually more valuable than 5 000 views with a CTR of 0.2, even though they both generate the same traffic. On the other hand, achieving 10 000 views will cost you more than achieving 5 000 views.

The goal of SEO

More Google views means more visitors to your website, and more visitors means more purchases. That's a common truth among SEO people. But it's a statistical truth. You need to take it apart and look at the constituent parts. In fact, the only Google users who are really important to you are the ones that you can convert into customers. What really counts is the number of "true conversions", as we saw above.

To sum everything up: The purpose of your SEO effort shouldn't stop at being visible in Google. Also, it shouldn't stop at attracting as many visitors as possible to your site. Your goal must always be to generate as many purchases as possible (whatever "purchase" means in your business).

A perfect SEO strategy

If you could somehow be visible only to Google users who will eventually turn into customers, and if you could make all of them click through to your site and make a purchase, then your SEO strategy would be perfect, in a way.

Of course, it can't be done. People will see your site and find it irrelevant. Others will not find it even though they would have liked it.

But until you reach the ideal place, at least you know what to aim for: Make your site visible for people who are inclined to purchase your products and turn those visitors into customers. SEO and conversion. No more, no less.

The SEO Equation

What we've said so far translates into a simple but important equation. For lack of a better name, let's call the SEO Equation:

Sales = Google Views x (Click Through Rate) x (Buy Rate)

Example: Increasing the buy rate by 10% while decreasing the number of Google views by 5% will increase the number of sales by 4.5%. The site gets less love from Google but works better for the visitors. (1.10 * 0.95 = 1.045.)

Actually solving the SEO equation is not trivial, of course. The number of views depends on the page's Google ranking for a great number of different search phrases. We can't predict these rankings with precision, and even if we could, the resulting number of views is largely unknown to us, and it varies from month to month.

Nevertheless, the equation will work as a guide for us, going forward. It's something to lean on mentally when considering your SEO efforts.

For each SEO decision you make, you should at least ask yourself: How does this affect each of the factors in the SEO Equation, and what is the total effect on my business? It is not unusual that a certain change will have a positive effect on SEO and a negative effect on conversion. You need to find the balance.

SEO – a machine with three levers

To make a website perform well in search engines, three areas need to be controlled:
- On-page SEO
- Technology
- Back links

On-page SEO

Most of this book will focus on the content that you publish on your site, and how to optimise it for the search engine – and for your readers. This is what we call on-page SEO. But before we get started, let's say a few words about the other areas as well.

Technology

The site must be built in a way that allows the search engine to see its content (it must be "bot accessible"). This is not difficult, but it's easy to go wrong. Also, things like the page's load time will affect its SEO value.

Back links

The centrepiece of Google's algorithm has always been about the links that point to a certain web page from other sites (external links, or back links). The more links that point to a page, the more relevant the page is deemed to be.

Each link to a page is seen as a vote for that page. This concept is still important for a website to rank well, and the top sites in competitive niches work hard to get a lot of links to their sites.

PS: Another kind of link is the **internal link**, which means a link from one page on your site to another page on your site. Internal linking is part of on-page SEO, and we'll be talking more about it later.

Now, let's focus on the main topic of this book, on-page SEO.

Introduction to on-page SEO

While some SEO techniques require you to reach out to the external world and deal with other people, on-page SEO consists of things that you can do yourself on your own website.

On-page SEO is all up to you, and if you fail, at least you know where the problem lies. (I won't spell it out for you.)

On-page SEO consists of three separate areas:
- Content
- Meta data
- Internal links

Content

Content is the text that you publish on your site. It's a short word but a huge area of expertise. This is where we will focus most of our on-page SEO efforts.

Meta data

Every web page consists of visible and invisible information:
- Visible information: the content that readers see
- Invisible information: information about the page

The invisible information is called meta data. It is data about the page and is separated from the data on the page (the content). The meta data is a very important part of on-page SEO, and we will be discussing it in detail.

Internal links

An internal link is a link from one page on your site to another page on your site. For example, your start page may contain links to other pages on the site. Or a page about a certain topic may contain links to pages with other, related topics.

Content – the backbone of the web

One thing is infernally good about good content: It will never be wrong.

Relevant and well-structured content will never go out of style on the world-wide web. No matter how you turn things around, no matter how Google changes its algorithm, content is what the web is about. Content is King!

I'm not saying good content will be enough to get you where you want to be (in the top positions of Google, or in a blooming web business). Other efforts will be required too.

But, if you do the content part correctly, it can never be held against you. Which is more than you can say about many other SEO techniques that have come and gone. History has proven it time and time again: Things that once looked smart turned out to be bad for you (after Google changed their algorithm).

This will not happen to good content. Since useful content is what web users are ultimately looking for, content will always be a good thing in the eyes of the search engines.

Finding your keywords

To produce content that is well optimised for the search engine, you must first figure out which search phrases, or keywords, to optimise for. Without this understanding, you're working without aim.

The first question is: "What will my potential visitors search for?" What do people type into Google when they look for a site like yours?

The answer to this question is what SEO people call "keywords". A more appropriate description might be "search phrases" or "keyword phrases" since they're not necessarily single words. We'll use all these designations throughout the book, meaning the same thing.

To answer the question, you shouldn't settle for your gut feeling – or any other person's gut feeling, for that matter (such as your boss's or your client's).

What is your page about?

To understand what your customers will type into Google when they want to find your web page (even though they don't know about it yet), you must figure out what the page is about. This shouldn't be too hard for you, since it is your page. Still, this step is often overlooked.

Sit down and think things through. Ask yourself the following question: "What will people search for when they need my product?"

Regardless of the purpose of your site, there are people out there who will eventually fulfil that purpose for you. Try and figure out what these people are most likely to type into Google when they start the voyage of becoming your customers. Or readers, or backers, or whatever it is that you want them to do.

Keyword analysis

To find a more reliable answer, you'll need to make a **keyword analysis**, and there are tools for this. We will not get into the specifics of these tools here. I often use Google's own tool for this. It is called Adwords Keyword Planner. It works for me, and it is free.

For each of your web pages, you need to figure out what is the most important keyword – the **primary keyword**. This is the phrase that you will be optimising the page for. You will also have a list of relevant search phrases that are somewhat less important – the **secondary keywords**.

Let's look at a real-world example of what this process might look like.

Example: The conference hotel

The owners of a conference hotel asked me and my colleague to search engine optimise their website. It was a really nice hotel down by the water, with beautiful facilities and a luxurious spa.

They had a website with beautiful, black-and-white photographs and nicely crafted texts about finding your peace and quiet, letting the soul catch up, and so on. Unfortunately, the site didn't get a lot of traffic, and that's why they called us.

To us, the explanation was obvious. Let's ask the question I mentioned above: What will people search for in Google when they are looking for a really nice conference hotel down by the water? Not surprisingly, we found that they search for things like "conference facilities", "meeting space", "seaside convention centre".

But when we looked at their website, we couldn't find one single mention of any such phrases. So, then, how would Google possibly figure out what the site was about?

There was all this beautiful language about peace and quiet, but let's be honest: What person responsible for booking a conference area would open up Google and type in "let soul catch up"? No one. Not a single one. And so, these people just wouldn't find this site. And the site didn't get any traffic. And it was all perfectly logical and fair.

For Google to show your site in its search results, it has to understand what the site offers. For whom it is relevant. And, for a computer script to be able to figure this out, the information you put on the site must be **explicit**. The text on your web pages must state clearly what the page is actually about. You can't expect Google to read between the lines. (Even though, admittedly, it is getting better at this too.)

Ranking your keywords

When you have a list of search phrases that relate to the web page you're optimising, you need to figure out which ones are the most important. A few factors come into play for each of the search phrases:

Search volume – how often the search phrase is typed into Google

Keyword relevance – how strongly the search phrase correlates to your web page

Search competition – the sites that show up in Google's top positions for this search

Search volume

The basic principle is to optimise your web pages for search phrases with large search volumes. You want to reach as many people as possible and maximise your web traffic. That's the basic premise, but we will have to modify it.

Before you optimise a web page for the biggest search phrase in the list, stop and think about the following factors.

Keyword relevance

First of all, how many of the people who type this search phrase into Google do you think are interested in your page? This is what we call keyword relevance, and there are a number of signs that should make you suspicious about a search phrase's relevance to your page.

Very generic phrases – Many of the people who type in "dog" in Google, 40 000 each month in my region, are not looking to buy dog food. A super generic search as "dog" span over so many different intentions, and even if I managed to dominate "dog" in Google, it would probably generate limited value for my dog food e-commerce site. I will not sell much dog food to people who Google for dog pictures, and so on.

On the other hand, the 390 monthly searches for "dog food online" should be very relevant for my page, and well worth optimising for. Even though it is a smaller search volume, it might generate more sales. At least in comparison to the cost of making my page rank for it. Optimising for this specific search phrase might be a better business decision.

Phrases with several meanings – Type the search phrase into Google and see what shows up in the search result. This will help you understand what meanings are included in the phrase.

When I was helping an online pharmacy optimising a page about mist (a moisturizing facial spray), I discovered that the biggest search phrase, "mist" itself, could mean a number of things, such as a TV series and an atmospheric phenomenon. This tells me that "mist" as a search phrase isn't very relevant for this web page. Many people typing "mist" into Google are not looking to buy facial spray.

Also, we would be competing with strong, authoritative sites such as Wikipedia and Imdb.com which means my SEO effort would likely not lead to a top position in Google. Again, more specific search phrases might be more valuable, such as "mist pharmacy", even though they have smaller search volumes.

This brings us to the last factor besides search volume and keyword relevance.

Search competition

Google's search results channel a lot of income to the websites of this world, and site owners are aware of this. In niches where the search traffic is particularly valuable, the competition for the top positions in Google is fierce.

Each search phrase is its own playfield, and SEO-savvy site owners play thousands of matches every day and every night, 24/7/365.

For example, if you would like to take a top position for a search term like "play online casino", normal day-to-day on-page SEO probably wouldn't be enough. It would take a big investment in content and backlinks and technology. It is much easier to compete for a small search phrase like "B&B in Stockholm archipelago", simply since no big players are established in this search niche.

Remember that Google is about domination. A very large proportion of the web traffic that passes through Google goes through the top positions. According to data from 2016, around 70 % of the clicks in Google's search results are awarded to the top five positions. You can read more here:

https://www.smartinsights.com/search-engine-optimisation-seo/seo-analytics/comparison-of-google-clickthrough-rates-by-position

Dominating many small searches may be more valuable than being a strong contender for very competitive search phrases but not quite making it onto the podium.

Don't be blinded by big numbers

Sometimes you will discover big search phrases that seem relevant to the subject area of your web page, still they are not for you. You should leave them alone, for business reasons and maybe for moral reasons too.

For example, when I was optimising a page selling headache pills, I discovered several big search phrases such as "headache cancer" and "constant headache". While the number of monthly searches were tempting and the page was indeed about headache, I'm sure those people were not looking for aspirin.

Even if we managed to dominate Google for "headache cancer", those searches likely wouldn't generate much sales. Instead, we would clog up the search results with sales messages, when in fact what these people need is expert advice.

Optimising pages with similar topics

As your website grows, or if someone hires you to work with a big website, certain topic areas will probably be covered by several pages. In this case, you need to optimise different pages for different search phrases, even if they treat similar topics.

For example, if you run a big recipe site, there may be ten or twenty recipes for grilled chicken. In this case, the keyword analysis we did for Señor Fefe's Pollo Loco may no longer be valid. If you already have a page that ranks well for "grilled chicken", you don't want to create another page to compete for the same primary search phrase. It would create internal search competition and your pages would start cannibalising on each other in Google. The new page would weaken the old page. In this case, you need to separate your pages SEO-wise by optimising them for different search phrases.

If a certain topic area has a lot of pages, you may want to create a hub page or list page where you list all the pages within that topic area. Then you can optimise the hub page for the major keyword phrase and save smaller and more specific search phrases for the sub pages.

Converting pages and supporting pages

All pages within your website are not equal. They have different purposes for your visitors. Some pages are there to sell products, others are used to give your customers information.

These different page types also play different roles in the "traffic generating SEO machine". While you want to optimise your highly converting landing pages for active, commercial search phrases such as "buy sneakers", information heavy pages can be optimised for less converting keywords, such as "children shoe sizes".

By building a hierarchy of highly converting and pages that are purely informative, you can catch both converting search phrases and information-seeking phrases. By equipping the latter pages with clearly visible links to the converting pages, they will support them in the hunt for converting search traffic. This is one reason why many commercial sites contain large sections with purely informational or educational content.

Once you have decided on a primary keyword and some secondary keywords for your web page, it is time to begin optimising your web page for the search engines.

Optimising content for search engines

The fate of your web page is largely decided by the content you put on it. Will it attract readers, or will it age in silence? Unless you drive traffic by advertising, it comes down to your visibility in the search engine.

The key to success with the search engine is to make it very clear what the page is about. This is done by putting clear and explicit text on the page. Google has acquired an impressive expertise in interpreting a mass of text, and every word you write counts.

But the Google algorithm is also instructed to put extra emphasis on specific parts of a text. These parts is where you should put your keywords.

H1 – the top-level heading

The most important element on the page in the eyes of Google is the H1 heading. Use your primary keyword in the H1, and you're on your way to world domination. (Even though some more work may still be required...)

Note: There is some evidence that the H1 has lost some of its dominance to rivals like H2 and maybe even H3. If for some reason you don't want to use H1, go ahead and use H2. Still I would recommend that you use H1 for your most important text element, and if this is impractical for some reason, change the site structure or the CSS to make it practical.

Smaller headings – use them!

It is not only H1 that counts. Using any heading format indicates that the text is important. Every heading on your page will trigger Google's sensitivity a little extra. The tips is to use more headings in your texts, and put more of your keywords in the headings.

Use your primary and secondary keywords in H2 and H3 elements, and Google will understand even better what you're about.

Tip: To maximise the SEO effect of a text, you should start using more headings. Quite possibly the most common malpractice by web owners and web editors is the omission of headings throughout their texts.

Please note that headings are not only used for whole pages or large sections on a page. Basically, each and every paragraph of the text on your page could profit from having its own heading, stating clearly what the paragraph is about.

In a sense, headings are like labels. They give the reader a quick hint what she can expect to find in the related chunk of text. Labels are a great tool for quick navigation and easy access to information.

When you start using headings properly, not only will you improve your SEO, you will also write texts with better readability and better conversion. But will talk more about that later, in the chapter on "Optimising content for readers".

The beginning of paragraphs

Another part of the page that gets extra weight in Google's algorithm is the beginning of each paragraph of text, most of all the first paragraph. Put your primary keyword in an early position in the first paragraph of your body text, and things will start looking bright for you despite your lowly beginnings.

Lists

Another element on the web page that gets extra love from Google is lists – bullet lists or numbered lists. Putting something in a list indicates an increased importance, and Google is aware of this. Use your keywords in list elements and Google will smile at you.

Emphasis

Just making a word bold gives it a little extra push in the search ranking. The page will perform somewhat better in search phrases containing the bold phrase.

This is also a way of introducing headings without hierarchy. Without a number like H4 or H5. When you go beyond two or three levels of headings, neither you nor your readers will be able to keep track of them anyway. It gets confusing.

Just put the least important headings in plain bold text. We might call these headings "labels", and like we said above, labels are a great way of increasing the readability, or availability' of the text, apart from strengthening the page's search ranking for certain phrases.

These simple techniques of using your keywords tactically on the page will take you a long way towards a search-optimised web page. Together with the keyword analysis, this is the core of on-page optimisation.

Interestingly, this way of structuring the text also works really well for readers. Which brings us to the next chapter.

Optimising content for readers

Now, after all this talk of writing for search engines, maybe you're thinking something like this:

"Hey, I write for my readers, my customers, not for some stupid computer script".

Well, good for you. You're absolutely right. Keep up the good work!

But please stay with me. I have a surprise for you. The way of structuring the text that we saw above, with the purpose of pleasing the search engine, you know what? It goes hand in hand with good readability and a good user experience! Let me explain!

The F-pattern

Are you familiar with usability guru Jakob Nielsen and his team? They use eye tracking to study how people read on the web. They have studied the way our eyes move over the screen when we try to extract useful information from a text on a web page.

What they found is this: When we read a web page, we typically start in the upper left corner, on the first words of the first sentence. We move along the line to the right for a bit, then down to a new paragraph or a new text element that grabs our attention, and again to the right for a short stretch.

When you let many people do this on the same web page, and you compile all these people's eye tracks into a "heat map", our habit of scanning the text for meaningful information results in a pattern that reminds us of an F. Or an extended F, seeing that there are typically more than two arms.

The result has been named "the F-pattern" because of the way it looks. You can read more about it here:

https://www.nngroup.com/articles/f-shaped-pattern-reading-web-content

Attractive text elements

When we scan a text for information, the text elements that attract our eye on its way down the text are typically one of the following:
- Headings and labels
- Beginning of paragraphs
- Lists
- Emphasized words

Does this look familiar? Where have we seen this list before? This is the exact same elements where I advised you to put your most important keywords when optimising your text for the search engine.

What a coincidence! Your readers and Google want the same thing! Amazing!

And, yes, it is amazing for real. Now you can keep writing for your readers while **at the same time** satisfying the needs of the search engine.

And maybe it's not really a coincidence. Maybe these two things are connected – human readability and search engine optimisation.

I don't know if one of them lies behind the other, or if there is a third factor lying behind them both. Most likely, the Google algorithm is trying to imitate human behaviour in its efforts to present relevant web pages in the search results.

Regardless of what comes first, this is very good news for us when we try to on-page optimise our web pages to meet the requirements of man and machine.

Example – essentials first

Let's say we have this old web page that isn't performing too well in Google. A situation that we would like to change. Before we do our on-page SEO magic, the first sentence of the page goes like this:

"Like my mother used to say, if a priest wants to make a really well-tasting paella, he should stop preaching and start cracking a few eggs, if he can have them cheap."

Okay, so let's analyse. What do we have here? We have an introductory sentence that starts with an anecdote about the author's mother.

Now recall the heat map of Jakob Nielsen that shows where the readers' eyes are looking for something relevant. The F-shape. What happens if you overlay that heat map on top of our example web page? I'll tell you what happens. In the hottest place of the whole page, we have put the following information: "Like my mother used to say."

Now, imagine you're at home with your kids and their little friends. They are constantly screaming and shouting and crying and laughing and demanding to get this and that and then refusing it when you bring it to them. Meanwhile, you're supposed to cook them a tasty and healthy meal before it's time to start the Gotobed War.

You google a nice and simple recipe for paella, but when you click to a page that looks promising, all you see is talk of someone's mother. "Bloody hell, I don't have time, let's try some other page!" Oops, you just lost a customer. Add one to your bounce rate.

Now, if instead you would re-phrase the first sentence a little, the future fate of your page might change radically.

"To cook paella, start by cracking a few eggs." Can you see what I mean? This text is more to the point. Essentials first. The stressed-out parent instantly recognizes a chunk of information that will solve his problem. He feels confident, and he stays on the page. Your bounce rate takes a hit. Yey!

I'm exaggerating here, a little bit, but only to make a point. The point is valid. This way of formulating things will make it so much easier for you reader to judge if she's come to the right place. And as a plus, Google will catch on as well and award you with a suitable ranking. Quite a big plus, unless you want your web page to be left in peace.

Caveat

Text is not black and white. Or, I mean... it may well be rendered in black and white, but it doesn't fit into a box. Or, I mean, even if it is black and white and fits into a box, text is, well, organic.

We use text to transfer thoughts between brains. They are separated in space-time, and since thoughts tend to be a bit fuzzy, the related text cannot always be modified to fit all the rules.

It is not always desirable to submit to all the principles of readability and search engine optimisation that we are establishing in this book. It is not always possible.

But if you deviate from these principles, at least do it consciously. Do it with good reason, after weighing in all the pros and cons. After applying the SEO Equation and visualizing the F-pattern.

Keyword density

As we mentioned above, for Google to figure out what a web page is about, you need to write it out explicitly. You need to tell Google what the page is about, at least once, or the purpose of the page will be lost on the Google algorithm.

But once may not be enough. You'd better tell it more than once. You'd better tell it a number of times.

Let's be honest, if a text mentions "video games" just once, would you think this is a text about video games? Probably not. At least, this is how Google reasons, and it makes sense.

In a text about cotton silk fabric, the main term "cotton silk fabric" would occur naturally a number of times. And this is what Google is looking for when they try to decide what the page is about.

It's called **keyword density**, or keyword frequency, and it is something you need to achieve in your text if you want your page to be visible in the search engine.

Once you've figured out which search phrases are the most important for a particular web page, you need to get these phrases into the text on that page with a certain frequency.

But don't overdo it. If you spam your text with your primary keyword, it will look unnatural. It's called "keyword stuffing" and it is something that Google sneers at. Keyword stuffing might even get your page penalised in Google's search results.

Make it natural, but don't neglect it. It's not about exact numbers.

Note: Reportedly, some evidence indicates that keyword density is no longer a ranking factor for Google's search ranking, or at least not as important as it used to be. Instead of repeating your primary keyword throughout the text, it is claimed, you should provide your text with variations of the primary keyword. Google has learned to read, and it will understand what the text is about.

While I believe this is partly true, I would recommend that you continue to think of your keyword density. Repeating the main phrase of a text can never be wrong. As long as it is done in a natural way, I'm sure it will not be penalized, just like relevant content will never go wrong. Then use variations of the keywords as well. Don't be afraid to change the form of the keyword phrases to make them fit into a natural text flow. It will strengthen your case even though it is not the original keyword phrase in its exact form. Will talk more about this in the section on "Using synonyms".

Increasing your keyword density

Take any of your existing web pages and I'm pretty sure you can increase the number of times that your primary keyword is mentioned on the page. There are a few simple tricks that go a long way when it comes to increasing the keyword density in a way that is perfectly natural.

Look out for "it" and "them"

Read through your text and look for occurrences of "it", "them" etc. Every time you find one of these words, ask yourself this: "What happens if I replace this word with the primary keyword?" If it looks good, do it.

After you run through the text looking for "it" and "them", your keyword density should have gone up considerably (see the example below).

Look out for omitted keywords

Ellipsis is a rhetorical trick that already the ancient Greeks knew about. It's when you say something without using all the words that you could have used.

For example, the sentence "I know how to cook a chicken, and you know how to cook a chicken too" could just as well be written as "I know how to cook a chicken, and so do you".

The sentence "I need to cook a chicken, but I'm not sure how to cook the chicken" could be shortened to "I need to cook a chicken, but I'm not sure how to."

Do you see how, in these examples, one mention of "chicken" disappears when you simplify the sentence? If your web page is about chicken, this simplification may not be in your best interest. It decreases the keyword density and makes it less obvious for Google that this is the world's most relevant page on how to cook chicken.

So, after you replaced some occurrences of "it" and "them" with explicit keywords, scan through the text and look for omitted keywords that you can replace with explicit mentions of your keywords. Your keyword density goes up, and your web business starts booming. Possibly.

Keep it natural

The last step in your keyword density effort is to smoothen the edges a bit. It's quite possible that you have overdone it. The text may have become a bit stiff and awkward.

To make things perfect, you might need to **take away** keywords in some places to achieve a good, readable text.

Once again, you must always avoid keyword stuffing, with consideration both to Google and to your readers. Keep the text natural and readable, but don't miss any chance of using a keyword phrase explicitly when it is natural. You will gain from it, and no one can ever punish you for doing this.

Example – increased keyword density

To get a better feeling for what keyword density means, let's look at three versions of the same text about cooking a chicken.

"Chicken" is our primary keyword here, and we want to increase the keyword density in this text. We'll replace a number of "it" as well as an omitted keyword.

Original text (1 mention of "chicken")

"Bring the water to a boil and cook the chicken well. Remove it from the pan, pull the meat apart with your fingers and put it in a bowl. You want to make sure you cook it well enough, but if it's still a bit pink inside it's ok, because later on we'll be adding it to the sauce."

Maximum keyword density (7 mentions)

"Bring the water to a boil and cook the chicken well. Remove the chicken from the pan, pull the chicken meat apart with your fingers, and put the chicken in a bowl. You want to make sure you cook the chicken well enough, but if the chicken is still a bit pink inside it's ok, because later on we'll be adding the chicken to the sauce."

Natural keyword density (5 mentions)

"Bring the water to a boil and cook the chicken well. Remove the chicken from the pan, pull the chicken meat apart with your fingers, and put it in a bowl. You want to make sure you cook the chicken well enough, but if the chicken is still a bit pink inside it's ok, because later on we'll be adding it to the sauce."

What do you think? Of course, this work always comes down to your feel for the language. How far can you stretch it without having a text that jumps up and hits the reader in the face?

Do you remember the SEO Equation? What you win in SEO, you may lose in conversion, and vice versa. It is a balancing act.

Using synonyms

One way of keeping the keyword density at a natural level while at the same time maximising SEO is to throw in some synonyms.

If you have used "the chicken" too often, you may want to replace it with "the bird", "the meat" or even "the food" in well-chosen places.

Not only does this lend a natural flow to the language, without exaggerated repetitions, it also helps Google understand what the text is about. Google has become increasingly "intelligent", and today it is safe to say that Google knows how to read. Google will pick up the purpose of your page from synonyms to the most important keyword phrases too.

Long tail effects

Also, by using synonyms for the most important keywords, the page will catch a broader array of searches.

Less common search phrases, phrases that fewer people type into the search engine, are called **long tail**.

Each long tail search phrase in itself doesn't generate much traffic, but long tail phrases come in huge numbers, and there's less competition for them compared to the bigger, more commercial keywords.

Catching a wide range of long tail searches is a cheap effort, and it adds to your bottom line.

Keywords and side words

So, you've put your primary keyword first (or early) in the H1 heading. What about the rest of the words in the heading? Should you try and replace these words too with keywords that are more frequently used in searches? Probably not.

These "side words" in the heading do not function as keywords. They are not supposed to match any particular search phrases. Instead, the purpose of these side words are more related to information. Clarity. Conversion. In this place, it is probably better to write your best God damn sales prose.

Example – keywords and side words

Let's say you've been asked to search engine optimise a recipe for grilled chicken. The suggested headline (from the friendly and competent chef team) goes like this:

"Señor Fefe's Pollo Loco with chunky Mexican tomato salsa"

Now, according to our instructions, you start out with a thorough keyword analysis. And it points at some problems with this formulation.

First of all, the suggested heading doesn't really say what it is about.

Even if your Spanish is decent and you recognize "pollo" for chicken, from this headline you cannot figure out how this chicken is prepared.

This heading is so far from your normal SEO standard that you actually have to phone down to the kitchen team and ask them what Señor Fefe's Pollo Loco is all about. "What, why?" they tell you, "It's our spicy peanut grilled chicken, dude!"

"Okay, then I understand. Saludos, I have work to do."

Let's try a new version:

"Spicy peanut grilled chicken with chunky Mexican tomato salsa"

Now that's better. At least now you can figure out what's for dinner. Or, more to the point, this heading contains keywords that someone might actually search for in Google.

No one will ever search for Señor Fefe's Pollo Loco – except possibly señor Fefe himself, but he's not your customer. He's your employer. Maybe.

Still, our problems are not over yet. With a renewed keyword analysis, you realize that there are very few searches for the phrase "spicy peanut grilled chicken" (too few to measure at the time of this writing). Meanwhile, the more generic phrase "grilled chicken" is typed into the Google search box 90 000 times every month.

So, for primary keyword we should probably go with the often searched for phrase "grilled chicken". It is also highly relevant for this web page, since it's a recipe for grilled chicken. When a user sees "grilled chicken" in the search result's blue link, it will have a certain interest for her. We have a large search volume coupled with relevance, and it is hard to turn down this opportunity for added search traffic, even though the chef team may get a bit grumpy.

New version:
"Grilled chicken in spicy peanut marinade with chunky Mexican tomato salsa"

Now the primary keyword has been taken care of. It's in prime position and Google will give it its sweet, sweet love.

What about the rest of the heading? Again, our keyword analysis tells us that the phrase "chunky Mexican tomato salsa" isn't something people type into Google very often (too few hits to be measured). The more generic "chunky salsa" gets 1,600 searches every month. Maybe we should use this instead? Not necessarily. Because now we're dealing with the side words.

Even though "chunky salsa" is decisively more searched for than "chunky Mexican tomato salsa", it is probably not a search phrase that you want this page to rank for.

Why is that? Short answer: because the phrase is not relevant for the page.

Imagine a thousand people firing up Google and typing in "chunky salsa". How many of these are looking for a recipe of grilled chicken?

Not many, I'd say. So, even if you should manage to rank in Google for "chunky salsa", few users would click out to your site from Google. Also, whatever traffic you *did* get would be full of bounces when people realised your page is actually about chicken.

So, instead of search engine optimising the "side words" in your headings, it is probably better to use them for converting readers. Remember, SEO and conversion go are two links in the same chain.

Rather than search engine optimising the side words, use selling, or nice, or funny, language for the rest of the heading after the keywords. Make it sound really good to your readers, and maximise the number of visitors to your site that have a genuine interest in your content.

In this case, you might want to lean on the market understanding of your chef team and keep the lovely "chunky Mexican tomato salsa" as is.

In the end, again, it comes down to a guess work where you try to balance search ranking and (true) conversion. It's a great adventure!

Optimising meta data

A web page consists of visible text, which is the ordinary content, and "invisible" text, text that is not displayed on the page. The invisible text is called meta data, since it is data about the page rather than data on the page. The meta data is visible in other places, and it plays an important role for on-page SEO.

Meta data in this context consists of two parts:
- The html title
- The meta description

Html Title – important for both SEO and conversion

The <title> element of an Html page is pretty much what it says - it's the page title.

The page title is displayed in two important places:
- In Google's search results - this is the legendary blue link!
- In the top bar of the browser window

The top bar of the browser window is not important for us, but the importance of the blue link in Google's search results cannot be overstated. The blue link is a central piece of text – for both SEO and conversion purposes.

SEO: The first words of the Title element are highly valued by Google's ranking algorithm. It's a piece of your "web estate" that you should populate with great care. Neglecting this is potentially a great loss of monetary value to your business.

Conversion: The text in the blue link will greatly impact Google users' choice to click on your link or not.

RULE: Unless you have a very good reason, the Title element should contain your web page's primary keyword, preferably in an early position.

Example – Html Title

If you look at web pages all around the internet, you'll see that many of them don't follow the rule that we just. Often enough, the Title begins with the company name, or a friendly but useless "Welcome".

Remember the million dollar question: Would your "true converts" fire up Google and search for "welcome"? Well, your question is your journey.

Meta description

The meta data element called "meta description" is in reality a <meta> element with its Name attribute set to "description". But that's a technicality and we need not bother with it here. We'll call it the meta description, as is the custom in the SEO business.

The meta description is an important piece of the on-page SEO puzzle, and you should put solid work into it. But unlike the Html Title, this is lawless land with unpredictable behaviour and no hard-coded rules.

Where is meta description used?

Meta description is often described as the text that is displayed below the blue link in Google's search result. As such, it plays an important role for the conversion of Google users into visitors of your site.

TIP: The description text below the blue link is a free ad space in the search engine. Use it to the maximum! You have approximately 160 characters to bring out a message to the people who will be buying your products.

However, it is not always true that your meta description will be used in the search result. As a matter of fact, it is quite rare. Or, more correct, the text below the blue link is almost never identical to the page's meta description. But it may contain snippets of the meta description, and you have some tools to control this.

Description text constructed on the fly

When a search result is presented to a Google user, the description below the blue link is constructed on the fly. For this purpose, Google reserves the right to use whatever text content is can find on your page that seems relevant to the search in question.

If the meta description seems relevant to the search phrase that the user typed in, Google may use the meta description, or part of it. But if Google finds a more relevant text passage anywhere on your page, this text may show up below the blue link instead.

Given the number of possible search phrases that people may conceivably type into Google to find your page, it is obviously impossible to design a meta description text that is relevant to them all, not least when you're limited to 160 characters. So what to do?!

Use your keywords

Let's go back to the keyword analysis. Do you remember that we tried to figure out which search phrases people will use most often in relation to the web page? These became our main keywords for the page, and now they come to use again.

By using the most important search phrases in the meta description, you will maximise the chances that parts of the meta description is used in Google's search results.

Caveat: Even if you use your primary keyword in the meta description, there is no guarantee that your skilfully crafted text will actually be displayed in Google. In my experience, it is very hard to control Google's behaviour on this point.

Other uses for the meta description

Contrary to Google, other sites often use the meta description verbatim. When people share your site on Facebook or other social sites, your meta description is often used to present the page.

Conclusion

This is what you need to understand about the meta description:

SEO: Meta description doesn't affect the page's Google ranking, in contrast to the Title element which is essential for SEO.

Google snippet: There's no guarantee that the meta description will be used in the search result. Google will use any snippet of relevant text that it can find on your page and put it below the blue link.

Social: Your meta description may be used when sharing the page in social media.

All things considered, your best bet may be to craft a meta description that presents the page in a good way and reads well in itself, as a whole. And if you throw in one or two keywords, parts of the meta description may be used now and then in Google's search results and play a role for your conversion rate.

Meta Keywords – not to be used

The meta keywords tag is a piece of meta data that used to be important for SEO purposes. Ten years ago, Google used keywords to figure out what the page was about, But with the increased intelligence of the Google algorithm, the meta keywords tag has been abandoned. It is not being used any more. You should just save your energy and ignore it.

Search Engine Friendly URLs

The web page's web address may carry some weight in Google's assessment of the page's relevance for the search in question. If you use the page's primary keyword in the page url, this may help the page rank well in Google.

Update: This is an area where things may be changing. According to some evidence, the url no longer weighs into a page's Google ranking. But, as far as I know, the evidence is not conclusive. Also, a relevant url has other advantages. It makes the site structure easier to figure out and may improve your visitors' user experience. Plus, there's certainly no evidence that an incomprehensible or confusing url improves the page's Google ranking either. So let's stick to relevant and legible url:s for the time being

Optimising internal linking

Internal linking is how you link between pages on your website. It is the opposite to external linking, which means links to your website from other sites.

Internal linking is a key factor for your web pages' Google ranking. It is something you need to work with regularly and wisely.

Internal links can be found in the site's menus, but more importantly in the body text on your web pages. The links work as references to other pages with related topics. This kind of cross reference is a traditional way to broaden and deepen the reader's understanding of the subject.

Optimising your text links

Links are important for both your visitors and the search engine. By linking between related pages, you may increase the usability of your site. Links make it easier for visitors to find the information that they are looking for. But an internal link may also improve the Google ranking of the page that it is pointing at.

If a page on your site gets links from many other pages on the site, this shows Google that the page is important. This is something that Google will catch up on and reward with improved ranking for the page.

Link important search phrases – sometimes

Apart from a designated target page, each link also consists of an anchor text. It is simply the text that users will click on to follow the link. It is the text that is blue and underlined if the page follows the original web design.

By using the target page's keyword phrases in anchor texts for links that point to that page, you will strengthen its ranking for those keywords. You're making it clear to Google what the target page is about, and Google rewards clarity.

But, like many other things, this should not be overdone. There is a risk in overdoing this. If you work too aggressively with "keyword spamming" anchor texts, the search engine may even punish your site, simply by ignoring the internal links.

If you create a lot of internal links from pages across the site to a certain page, make sure to use a variation of anchor texts. Let some anchor texts be completely unrelated to your overall keyword strategy. Throw in some "naive" links, such as "click here" or "read more". Your site will have a natural link profile that doesn't raise the search engine's suspicions.

Also, with the increasing competence of the Google algorithms, the search engine can pretty much figure out what it is all about by interpreting the context where the link is placed. Google knows how to read!

TIP: If you use keywords in the Title attribute of the <a> element, this will also strengthen the impact of the link on the target page's Google ranking.

Use a sensible amount of links

Internal links are important, but again you should avoid over-using them. First of all, too many links may make the page look messy to the reader. Readability goes down, along with trust and buy rate.

It also won't do you any good in the struggle for top spots in Google. If a page has a lot of outbound links, each link will have less impact. The page's total "link power" is distributed over all outgoing links. The largest chunk of link power is funnelled through the first link on the page, and then each successive link gets a little less.

So, don't spray your pages with links. A common recommendation is to use no more than 3 to 5 links on each page. Focus on links that are relevant to the text where you place them, while keeping your SEO strategy and your keyword analysis in mind.

TIP: Some internal links will be pointing to pages that you don't want to give any extra search strength, such as "About us" or your FAQ. You could mark up these links with the "nofollow" attribute to make Google ignore them.

Then they won't be stealing any search energy from your top pages that are out there in cyberspace fighting for attention.

Balancing link power and conversion

On pages that have a clear purpose of converting your visitors, for example into buying your product or click out to your partner's site, you may want to reduce the number of outgoing links. Each link that leads away from the page gives visitors an easy way out. The rate of people leaving the page without taking action tends to go up. In this case, search optimisation stands against conversion. As always.

Also, on those "landing pages", you may want to use anchor texts that are as converting as possible, rather than focused on SEO. For example, a call-to-action phrase like "Buy now" or "Click here" might be preferred to a keyword-centric anchor text such as "cheap running shoes".

Analysis and adjustment

Have a little patience

Sometimes, the optimisation of a web page takes effect right away. As soon as Google finds your changes and exposes them to the algorithm, your page may suddenly figure in top positions for a number of search phrases. It is a great feeling, and it will affect your business in a positive way.

Sometimes, though, the effects on your ranking are not as quickly visible. Many, many factors are weighed into the search ranking for every individual page, particularly for big sites, and you may have to make adjustments in many places before you can detect any significant improvements to your rankings.

Request indexing by Google

When you update your web page, it will take a while before Google finds your changes. Depending on how much traffic the page gets, it may happen overnight or it may take days or even weeks before it happens.

To quicken this process, you may ask Google to index the page. For this, you use a Google function called "Fetch as Google". You can read more about it here:

https://support.google.com/webmasters/answer/6066468

Once you have requested indexing, it is usually a matter of minutes or hours before your changes have been updated in Google's search results and start effecting the page's ranking.

Day to day variations

If you look at the statistics for your site, or some page on your site, you will probably see a jagged curve. Traffic can change quite a lot from day to day, it is the normal state of affairs.

But when you try to figure out if your optimisation of a page has had any effect, this jaggedness of the data is a problem. If traffic went up after your changes, it may be just a normal variation. If traffic went down, it also doesn't mean that the changes were a failure. Often, you need to gather data for a certain time before any traffic changes become obvious.

Improved ranking does not imply increased traffic

If traffic changes may take a while to detect, improved search ranking is often more "digital". First, your page rank as #100, then it ranks as #25. Even if the ranking varies a little from day to day or hour to hour, a change like that is often easy to establish.

However, improved ranking does not mean that you will get more traffic to the page. A crushing majority of clicks in Google's search results are centred around the top positions. A very small share of searchers flip to subsequent pages of the search result and clicks on a blue link in position 15 or 25. This explains why a leap from #100 to #25 probably doesn't change much for your traffic. No one clicks on position 100, and no one clicks on position 25. You improved your ranking, but not your traffic.

SEO is about domination, and if you can't reach a top position for a certain search phrase, you may want to chose to optimise for an easier one.

On-page SEO is an ongoing effort

Search engine optimisation should be a natural part of your process when creating new pages or blog posts on your site. Never forget your keyword analysis. Always consider your internal linking strategy before you mark a new page as Done in your To Do list.

You will also need to go over the site regularly and brush up your SEO. Your understanding of the site and the importance of the individual pages will change over time. Also, the importance of the individual pages as such will change over time.

The world changes, and being in the right place is an ever continuing effort. I hope you enjoy it!

Conclusions

As you see, on-page SEO is not magic, even though it may feel like magic when you see your web pages surge up the ladder of popularity in Google. Rather than magic, it is a craft that can be carried out by following a number of instructions and applying your understanding of your visitors.

SEO is not only about attracting web visitors. It is about understanding how people structure their understanding of reality. More specifically, SEO is about how your customers structure their understanding of the niche you're active in.

If you notice that certain search phrases are often being used, it tells you that this is how people think of these things. It gives you good reason to structure your information accordingly. So, when you craft web pages based on a keyword analysis, you're not only fishing for love from Google, you're structuring your information according to people's expectations.

To write texts that satisfy both humans and machines, you need to bring out your best writing. And that's what you want to do, isn't it? Have fun with it!

***

Copyright - About the Author

Copyright ©2017 by Lars Sundin

*

Lars Sundin is a Stockholm based writer with long experience from producing web copy and technical information for companies such as Nasdaq/OMX, Ericsson, IBM, PokerListings.com, IconMedialab and others. His educational background in physics and mathematics makes him well positioned to grasp the analytical and data driven aspects of search engine optimised web copy.

*

Thank you to Topdog, Curamando, Defiso, WGP and others for giving me the chance to learn by doing.

***